EGYPTIAN MYTHOLOGY FOR KIDS

DISCOVER FASCINATING HISTORY, FACTS, GODS, GODDESSES, BEDTIME STORIES, PHARAOHS, PYRAMIDS, MUMMIES & MORE FROM ANCIENT EGYPT

HISTORY BROUGHT ALIVE

FREE BONUS FROM HBA: EBOOK BUNDLE

Greetings!

First of all, thank you for reading our books. As fellow passionate readers of History and Mythology, we aim to create the very best books for our readers.

Now, we invite you to join our VIP list. As a welcome gift, we offer the History & Mythology Ebook Bundle below for free. Plus you can be the first to receive new books and exclusives! Remember it's 100% free to join.

Simply scan the QR code to join.

Keep up to date with us on:

YouTube: History Brought Alive

Facebook: History Brought Alive

www.historybroughtalive.com

CONTENTS

INTRODUCTION

Ancient Egypt. You might not know specific facts, but

I am sure you have already heard about these: pyramids and mummies. Am I right? Well, surprise, these things are two of the most known characteristics of an old civilization called Ancient Egypt! Before it became the country it is today, in the North of the African continent, Egypt went through a lot of events, especially in the years known as "B.C.," which means Before Christ. That's right! These things happened way before the birth of Jesus, which was more than 2000 years ago. That is how old Egypt is.

You may not know a lot about Ancient Egypt, but this book is here to help you solve that problem—I have united all of the most important points of that period and will show you how awesome they were. Don't believe me? Well, let me tell you what you can expect from this book (let me go ahead and say: a little bit of everything).

You will learn about the Egyptian kingdoms and the pharaohs who ruled them. Did you know that a pharaoh is a name given for the queen or king of Ancient Egypt and that they wore some cool crowns that had the image of a snake on them? Well, they were the most powerful people in the kingdom, so I guess it was alright for them to wear whatever they wanted.

In this book, you will also read about what life was like in Ancient Egypt and what made it so special. I will give you a tip: it is related to the Nile River. The Nile is the longest river on earth, and it is home to hippopotami and crocodiles. Of course, the Egyptians were scared of them, but I will tell you more about it later.

And guess what: there are many stories that used to be told at the time and myths about gods and goddesses (and a particular surprise story, wait and see) that will help you understand everything they believed in. There is a small section on who the main gods were and what they represented. Ancient Egypt also had some mythical creatures, and they were really cool, too.

There is also a part in this book that talks about something that was very important to the Egyptians, which is death and what happened after you died. But do not be scared or worried, it was something that belonged to their culture, and we need to tell you about it so you understand them better. Just so you can see how important death and the afterlife were to them, it is related to the mummies, the pyramids, the temples, and writing. I know, it's crazy, right? How can people like death this much? It is not fun at all. Or maybe they thought it was; you have to read to find out.

Finally, there is a super special section of the significant inventions of the Egyptians. Can you believe that we still use some of them today? I will not tell you what they are right now, but could you try to guess? When you get there, you will be able to see if you got it right or not. You will see that the Egyptians were really smart people and that their inventions helped them and are still very useful to the present day.

Did I make you curious? I hope I did so you can read on! This book has answers to all of the questions about Ancient Egypt and more! Sit tight and enjoy the ride. You are in for some real fun! See you at the end!

CHAPTER 1
KINGDOMS

Ancient Egypt refers to the place that is known today as the country of Egypt, in the North of the African continent. The people who lived there were known as Egyptians, and they still are! Before it was one country, Egypt was divided into two: Upper (in the South, known as White Land) and Lower (in the North, known as Red Land) Egypt. However, a King came by around 3100 B.C. and decided that he would join both parts of the country so it would become one. When that happened, the period known as Ancient Egypt started.

Before King Menes, Egypt was in what historians know as the Predynastic Period. Predynastic means that it was before the dynasties, which is when the rulers' children became kings or queens after their parents. Ancient Egypt existed for more or less 3000 years, and it was huge! It had many ups and downs and kings and queens during this time. It existed until the Romans invaded the country and took power.

In this chapter, you will learn about the different kingdoms that existed in Ancient Egypt.

Predynastic Period (6000 B.C.–3100 B.C.)

During the Predynastic Period, something really important happened in Egypt. People stopped hunting animals and started growing their food by using the water of the second largest river in the world, the Nile. They also stopped hunting animals and started to domesticate them. This means they would not go out to look for their food, but they would have the animals controlled near them to provide what they needed. Because this was a very, very long time ago, there is very little information about this time. However, Egyptologists, which is the name of those who study Egypt, found objects and drawings that helped them understand what happened at the time.

Life in Upper Egypt

Like I said before, Egypt was divided into Lower and Upper Egypt. While excavating the area where this was, archaeologists were able to find lots of cool things that tell them the story of the place. For example, they know that the White Land (another name for Upper Egypt) was home to the Badarians and their main city was Nekhen. They were able to understand this through drawings that were made in rocks, which people did to tell stories. This is the beginning of the Egyptians' writing, known as hieroglyphics.

Something else that these drawings told the historians is that the people in Upper Egypt lived in tents! This is probably because they needed to move around, and it is easier to carry a tent than build their own house (it is also faster). However, they found out that the Egyptians changed from living in tents to living in homes made of bricks dried by the sun during this time. This probably happened because now they grew their own food and didn't need to move around as much.

Archaeologists in this area have also found some pretty neat objects from the time, like ceramic pottery, jewelry, and tools that the Egyptians used. Finally, they also discovered something that is very common today: the use of cemeteries.

Before, when their loved ones died, they would be buried near their family's home. However, during this time, Egyptians started using cemeteries to bury those who died.

Life in Lower Egypt

Do you know how the Badarians lived in Upper Egypt? Well, the North of Egypt was home to another population: the Faiyum A. They lived near the delta of the Nile River, which is where the river finishes and sends its water to another body of water. Historians believe that since there was more water and more resources in this area, the people in Lower Egypt were more developed and had more money. It even had a capital named Memphis.

One cool thing to know is that it was in Lower Egypt that the first forms of government were developed. The land was divided into tribes, and each tribe had its leader. There was also one leader that was responsible for all of the other leaders. Archaeologists have discovered some exciting things about these people. Remember how I said that they started farming and growing their own food? Well, excavations have discovered that the people in this area built places to store their food, which is pretty advanced for them. Plus, these structures were both above and underground. Can you imagine? They also did ceramic work and made baskets.

8

Finally, it was in Lower Egypt that they discovered what type of animals the Egyptians were domesticating. Can you guess what they were? No? Well, don't worry. I will tell you: they were sheep and goats!

Early Dynastic Period (3100 B.C.–2686 B.C.)

Like I said before, King Menes unified Egypt and, with him, began what historians call the First Dynastic Period. King Menes was a really smart guy, and so when he saw that Lower Egypt was more developed than Upper Egypt, he decided to establish the new capital of the country there, near the Nile, of course. He gave it a really nice name: White Walls.

But something also happened in the religion of the country. People started believing that the king had superpowers and they could talk to the gods. They started thinking that the king was on Earth to be the interpreter for what the gods wanted. How do we know this? Well, during this time, the first hieroglyphics were written, and this has allowed historians to learn more about the time.

The Early Dynastic Period had three dynasties: the First, the Second, and the Third—all from related but different families. And that is a lot of people! For example, the First Dynasty lasted 260 years and had no less than six different kings.

There is also something really cool about this time. Something really important happened. I will give you a clue: there were great advances in culture, technology, and architecture. Can you guess what was so important that happened at this time? Well, if you guessed that the first pyramid was built, you are right! The first pyramid was built during the Third Dynasty, near the end of the Early Dynastic Period. They also developed the calendar during this time, and their writing got more elaborate, allowing researchers to have more information about the time.

Old Kingdom (2575 B.C.–2130 B.C.)

After the Early Period, a new time started in Ancient Egypt. This period was known as the Old Kingdom, and it lasted for a long 445 years! During this time, Egypt had the Fourth, Fifth, and Sixth Dynasties, with more kings and queens. But the most important thing about this time was that it was when the most pyramids were built. For example, the Great Pyramid of Giza and the Sphinx were constructed during this time. Because of this, this period is known as "the period of pyramid builders." We will see a lot more about the pyramids further along in the book, so hold onto your horses, and we will get there!

Another thing that happened during this time, more specifically during the Fifth Dynasty, was that the Egyptians started worshiping a new god. The God of the sun, Amun-Ra. Because of this, the priests began having more power, although they still answered to the king. But it was not only the priests that had more power. The generals in the military and the nobles also started having more influence and government participation. Finally, when a king who was not so smart took power at the end of the sixth dynasty, the people saw that he was not very good, so they took him out of power. A new period started in Egypt, known as the First Intermediate Period.

The First Intermediate Period (2181 B.C.– 2055 B.C.)

The First Intermediate Period had four dynasties—the Seventh, Eighth, Ninth, and 10th. There were many rulers during this time because there were a lot of wars in Egypt, so the kings and queens kept changing. What was once a territory with one king who had all the power now were separate territories with different governors, and one kept trying to invade the other. There was also a big problem with people from outside of Egypt trying to invade the country. All of this led to the economic and political weakness of the country.

The Middle Kingdom (2056 B.C.–1786 B.C.)

After all the mess that Egypt lived through during the first intermediate period, it was finally in the Middle Kingdom that a king finally reunited the country. This king belonged to the 11th dynasty, which lasted for only one king, who was later killed. A new king started to rule the country when that happened, and the 12th Dynasty began.

During this time, Egypt had a really strong military and started invading other countries. They wanted to get more goods and more money, so they tried to attack all of the kingdoms nearby that they thought had these things. However, by the 13th Dynasty, Egypt lost control of most of the territories it had conquered. There were also a lot of people arriving in the country, especially from Asia. With this loss of power, the country was weak again and separated into different territories, bringing what was known as the Second Intermediate Period.

The Second Intermediate Period (1786 B.C.– 1567 B.C.)

The first thing that happened during the Second Intermediate Period was a change in the capital of Egypt—it was transferred from Memphis to Thebes. Also, during this time, different dynasties existed at the same time since each one controlled a different territory. However, this made Egypt a weak country and allowed it to be invaded by a foreign civilization: the Hyksos, who got power but maintained most of the Egyptian cultures and traditions.

Everyone lived in peace until the leaders of Thebes decided it was time to reunite the country. They kicked the Hyksos out of Egypt and regained control of the country. They finally reunited the North and the South with the Middle land, which led to a new period in Egyptian history.

New Kingdom (1567 B.C.–1085 B.C.)

During the period of the New Kingdom, Egypt became an empire. This means that it controlled many territories, and these were from the northeast of Africa to other countries such as Syria, Babylonia, Palestine, and Assyria. It was also during this time that Egypt had some of its most famous kings—can you guess which ones they were? If you said Tutankhaum and Amenhotep, you are right! Because of the reach that the Egyptian empire had in other countries, trade went really well for them, and they were able to get many objects from different places in the world.

Something really curious happened during this time, which was the Ramesside period. It had this name because there were 11 kings named Ramses, one right after the other. Although it has a curious name, this period was a good one for Egypt, since the kings gained more importance and religious messages were written on the walls of temples. These temples were huge—they had to be big and beautiful to honor the kings and the queens.

However, although this was a really positive time for Egypt, by the time that King Tutankhamun took power, it had lost most of the territories of its empire, which led to a Third Intermediate Period in the country's history.

The Third Intermediate Period (1085 B.C.– 664 B.C.)

Because of the challenges brought by the loss of territory, there were great changes in most aspects of Egypt's culture, society, and government. The government once again spread out and gave space for the 21st to the 26th Dynasty. Something different was going on, where one part of the territory was ruled by a king and another by priests.

It is known that there were kings from another country named Libya during this period and that Egypt had lost almost all of the territories it had conquered during the New Kingdom. Most of the Egyptian traditions were left aside by the different origins of the rulers. Syrians and other territories invaded Egypt and tried to force their culture onto the locals.

The Late Period (664 B.C.–332 B.C.)

Egypt was so weak that other countries kept invading them, particularly the Persians, who were quickly expanding their territory. They stayed in Egypt for more or less 100 years until the last of the native kings came to power, from the 28th to the 30th Dynasties. In trade, the Egyptians started trading more with the Greeks, who were close to them through the

Mediterranean Sea, and because of this, many of them came to live in Egypt.

Since the Greeks were people who loved to write, something really interesting happened during this time: Several writers from Greece wrote down what they saw during their trips to Egypt. This is really cool because it provides us today with a lot of the information we have about the time.

The kings also started to do a lot for Egypt, focusing more on their own land rather than trying to expand. Because of more internal focus on the part of the kings, the economy and the culture started to revive. One of the main characteristics of the period is the increase in animal worship, which reached its peak during the Late Period.

Unfortunately, all that is good came to an end. This period lasted for only about 60 years when Persia once again invaded Egypt and was taken from power by Alexander the Great from Macedonia.

Macedonian and Ptolemaic Period (332 B.C.– 30 B.C.)

After the invasion of Alexander the Great, the military in Egypt was divided and, after his death, began the Ptolemaic rule, a family of nobles to whom Egypt was conceded after the division of the empire by his generals. Their descendants ruled Egypt until the death of Cleopatra in 30 B.C. The queen, who was known for being extremely capable and an ambitious ruler, stayed in power until the Roman invasion and is, still today, the most famous female ruler of Ancient Egypt.

CHAPTER 2
GEOGRAPHY

If I asked you to point out Egypt on a map, would you be able to do it? Egypt is located in the North of the continent of Africa, and it has three water sources: the Mediterranean Sea, the Red Sea, and the Nile River. To its left is Libya, and to the south is the country of Sudan. Today, the country's capital is Cairo, which is located very, very close to the Great Pyramids of Giza.

Egyptologists say that invading Ancient Egypt was hard because of its geography. On two of its sides are water bodies, and on the two others, there is the desert. No one was crazy enough to walk through the desert heat for days to attack them, so it provided the country with natural protection. To protect them even more, to the south of Egypt, there is a chain of mountains, which also help to protect the territory.

However, it would be impossible to talk about Ancient Egypt without talking about the Nile. The river provided, and still provides, the Egyptians with everything they needed—from a water source for farming to a means of transportation. After the Nile flooded, it left the land just right to plant the seeds. The land that results from the Nile floods is called kemet, or black land. Meanwhile, the Egyptians also had a name for the hot, dry land of the desert: it was called a *desert*, or red land.

The Nile

Did you know that the Nile is the longest river in the world? Well, it is! It also has three branches and six waterfalls. These branches are called the White Nile, the Blue Nile, and the Atbara River. The three branches are important because they provided the Ancient Egyptians with water for farming, especially the Blue Nile with its floods. Because the water from the river gave them a way to grow their food, the Nile was seen as a symbol of life by the Egyptians, contrary to the desert that exists on the other side of the country. It is also the reason why many of the cities in Ancient Egypt developed near the river.

The Nile was so important to the people in Ancient Egypt that their calendar was built according to the cycle of the river—its floods and droughts. The Egyptians had specific names for each of the three phases that the river went through. They were named according to each possibility that the river presented: the inundation season, Akhet; the growing season, Peret; and the harvest season, Shemu. Although today there is a dam to prevent the Nile from flooding, back in Ancient Egypt, the river used to flood for no less than six months, at the same period year after year. And because they were really smart, the Egyptians built canals leading to their crops coming from the Nile, which meant that they had water throughout the whole year to irrigate their crops.

Here is a curiosity for you: it was not only the river that was important but also the papyrus plants that grew around it. Although some people might just look at them as normal water plants, the Egyptians used them for a very important reason: to make something called papyrus, just like the plant itself was called. And do you know what papyrus was used for? Well, to make baskets, sheets, ropes, perfumes, medicine, and shoes, among many other things. One of them will probably surprise you: to make paper! Yes! Papyrus is the paper the Ancient Egyptians used to write on. They made scrolls and other documents with this type of paper, and it contains much of the information that we know about Ancient Egypt today.

Due to its proximity to water, the Egyptians also became experienced boatbuilders. They used the river to transport their people and goods, and for funerary reasons. However, the most important characteristic was the trade routes that it allowed the Egyptians to have—the other lands that they could access to sell their food and buy products from others.

The Mountains

The mountains in the South of Egypt protected them from possible invaders. After all, can you imagine climbing a mountain to attack another country with swords, shields, animals, and everything else that war requires? Well, because of this, the mountain barrier is considered an essential factor of protection to the Egyptians and made it possible for them to develop without much worry of an invasion from that region.

The mountains also played an important part in the flooding of the Nile. The reason for this is because every year when spring arrived, the snow that had fallen on the mountains would melt, and guess where all the water went to? You guessed right! The water would go to the Nile, and that would make the river flood.

The Desert

Egypt shares boundaries with two deserts: the Arabian and the Libyan deserts. Just like today, it was very rare to have people living there since there is almost no life—no animals to eat or hunt and little water to drink or to use to grow food. This is the main reason why Ancient Egypt developed near the Nile and not more centrally in the desert. It is estimated that more than 90% of Egypt is composed of deserts.

The Egyptian deserts are also known as the Western and the Eastern deserts, in reference to their location on the Nile River. In both, the climate is very hot and dry due to the lack of rain. There is almost no vegetation to be seen. However, they have caves, mountains, dunes, and bumpy areas.

Many historians say that the story of Egypt would have been entirely different if not for the desert. They believe that civilization would not have developed as it did. They also claim that the desert provided important things to the Egyptians, such as a specific type of sand they used to make glass. The constructions would also not be the same, as they would lack the primary resources to build them. Finally, history wouldn't be as preserved as it is today. This is because due to the lack of water and humidity, everything that was built a long time ago did not suffer too much decomposition and mostly remained intact. It would also be easier for invaders to access the country, increasing foreign influence.

The Mediterranean Sea

The Mediterranean Sea lies in the North of Egypt, which borders the country for almost 1000 kilometers. Some of the country's main cities are located along this coastline, and the same happened during the Ancient Egyptian civilization. Some of the country's main cities which still exist include Rosetta, Rafah, and Alexandria.

Although in the past, Egypt received goods from other countries that bordered the Mediterranean, a trade route was only established much later, near to the period in which Ancient Egypt existed. The participation of the Greeks was especially significant during this time. They traded products with the Egyptians and established a cultural trade. There are documents which tell about the visits of writers and researchers of the European country to the region, allowing a register of the period.

CHAPTER 3
LIFE IN ANCIENT EGYPT

Life in Ancient Egypt was very exciting. They always brought innovation from others and added new things to their culture. They had pets, art, agriculture, their own language, and way of writing. In this chapter, you will learn a little bit more about the aspects of the life of the Ancient Egyptians, and maybe you can find something that they did back then that you have now!

Government

Ancient Egypt had what historians call a theocratic monarch. This means that they had a king or queen and that they were both the leader of the country and the main religious leader at the same time. At that time, religion and government were one, even though the country's ruler was not a priest.

However, the priests were appointed by the ruler to take care of the temples of the gods.

To best understand the structure of the government they had at the time, I will teach you a trick: if it was called a kingdom, then there was only one ruler for the unified territory; if it was called an intermediate period, this means that the government was not central and that the power was spread among territories. Finally, when I mention empire, this means that they had territories not only in Egypt, but in other countries, and even continents.

Society

Ancient Egyptian society was very defined—there were the upper, middle, and lower classes. The pharaoh, or king, was on top of the pyramid as the most important person in society. After he or she came to the vizier, who was responsible for helping the king or queen rule. The vizier supervised the collection of taxes and was the second most important person in Egyptian society. Next came the landowners, government officials, military officers in high posts, priests, and doctors. The Egyptian middle class consisted of soldiers, merchants, artisans, and scribes. Finally, the lower class was composed of farmers and slaves. The farmers were responsible for taking care of the land for the owners and growing and harvesting crops for food. The slaves were generally prisoners captured in wars.

One important piece of information that you should know is that there was a very good legal system in Ancient Egypt—even enslaved people had rights. The social classes were also not delimited: This means a person from a lower social class could go up and be part of another social class if they studied, for example. Finally, you should know that, even though the Ancient Egyptian society was dominated by men, women also had rights—they could inherit the land and even divorce their husbands if they wished to do so.

Agriculture

As mentioned in the previous chapter, agriculture was extremely important for the Ancient Egyptians. It was, in fact, the most important economic activity of the country during this time. With the help of the Nile, they used to grow their own food and were also able to store it for periods of time with the development of better construction techniques. But what kind of food did they grow? Can you guess?

If you guessed wheat, barley, fruits, and vegetables, you are correct! These are precisely the main types of food grown by the Egyptians. Now, are you able to tell me what they are used for? Can you imagine what kinds of fruit were grown? Well, let's start with the fruits. Historians have identified the remains of watermelons, grapes, apples, peaches, pears, and figs as a part of the Ancient Egyptians' diet. They have also identified that they used wheat to make bread and barley for beer as a part of their daily diet. Other crops grown by them were onion, garlic, and lettuce.

Agriculture was also used for other purposes aside from producing food, such as making makeup, growing plants for medicine, and making fibers for clothes and shoes.

Animals

Did you know that animals were very important for the people of Ancient Egypt? They were used for several reasons: as pets, for food, for transportation, for cooking grease, for clothing, to help in farming, and for representing their gods! And don't think that the only animals they had as pets were dogs and cats. Oh no! They had hippos, crocodiles, hawks, and even monkeys as their pets. We can know all of this because of the drawings that were made inside the pyramids and some other stone-carved documentation. Maybe we should look a little closer at each of these animals and know what they were used for? Come on, let's go!

Cats

The cat was probably the most important pet in Ancient Egypt. Not only were they used as a pet, but they also gave their god Bastet the form of the cat. Therefore, it is safe to say that the Egyptians loved their cats very much. Egyptologists believe that almost every house in the kingdom had a pet cat, and, mind you, they could be big or small. The pharaoh, for example, had cheetahs and lions as pets, which symbolized the power that he had. Cats were also useful, as they kept the house clean and free from rats and other animals.

Dogs

Did you know that the Ancient Egyptians also had dogs as pets, like you might have one? Although they were mainly used as protectors of the house against invasions and were less frequent than cats, some Egyptians had dogs as pets. They were used for many reasons we still have around today: for hunting, protecting, helping the police, and for company, of course. Many pharaohs have been depicted in their tomb drawings hunting with their dogs or simply in their company. These animals were so important to the people that the

Ancient Egyptian god Anubis was represented as both a dog and a jackal.

Horses

Although the Egyptians did not have horses until the New Kingdom, they did have them, but not for the reason you are imagining. They did not ride the horses; they used them to help pull their chariots. The horses were used for war and hunting, but it was mostly the higher society that had them since they were expensive and complicated to look after. This means that there were very few horses in Ancient Egypt, but there were a significant number of mules, which were used to carry and transport materials.

Ibis

The ibis is a bird that was also used to symbolize an Egyptian god, Thoth. The Egyptians liked to observe birds in the wild but also raised them in captivity and used them as a way of making money.

Hippopotamus

Would you like to have a pet hippo? Well, let me tell you something—the Ancient Egyptians had hippos, but they were not nice at all! Hippopotami were not good pets because they were both scary and fascinating, especially when they were protecting their offspring. They are very aggressive animals who lived in the Nile and destroyed boats and attacked people who got near them. For this reason, it was not a good idea to have them as pets, although the Egyptians were so fond of them that they represented one of their gods in the form of a hippo—Taweret. In Pyramid drawings, the pharaohs are generally pictured fighting them. Today the hippopotami are extinct from Egypt and are considered the deadliest animal on the planet.

Crocodiles

Another animal that was very common in Ancient Egypt was the crocodile. Like the hippo, the crocodile was feared by the Egyptians. They were considered very aggressive and territorial and, therefore, more drawings of pharaohs fighting them can be seen in tomb drawings. The crocodile was also the representation of Sobek, a powerful god in Ancient Egypt known to take husbands away from wives.

Animals for Farming

Just like we have pigs, goats, and sheep today, the Ancient Egyptians also had them. They also had oxen for help with agriculture, chicken for their eggs, and cows for their milk. The skin of the sheep was used to make clothes, and the pigs were used for their fat. The Egyptians obtained meat and horns for decoration and artifacts from bulls and oxen, and they got their milk from cows and goats. Not very different from what we have today, isn't that true?

Writing

The language of Ancient Egypt is not very known, but have you ever seen their writing? You probably have, somewhere, since they are drawings that represent sounds and are called hieroglyphics, which means "sacred engravings" in Greek. This form of writing was used in tombs, temples, and pyramids, and written on stone and papyrus so that the Egyptians could spread a message, tell a story, or even reach the gods. Egyptologists have identified over 700 hieroglyphics, which can represent a sound, a situation, or a syllable—it is writing with a picture that is not a picture. Although the hieroglyphics are the most known form of writing in Ancient Egypt, they also had three other forms of writing: Hieratic, a form of cursive writing used by priests; Demotic, which was also cursive and used by people in general; and Coptic, the last stage of Egyptian writing adapted with Greek influence.

The Rosetta Stone

Have you wondered how historians know what was written in hieroglyphics if no one uses it anymore? I mean, take a look at an example of this writing and tell me what you can read... Absolutely nothing. However, a discovery made by the troops of Napoleon when they invaded Egypt has allowed this mystery to be deciphered. It is called the Rosetta Stone.

The Rosetta Stone was discovered in 1799 by French soldiers while they were repairing a fort in the city of Rosetta (thus, the name). The stone is a simple piece of rock that has some crucial information: It has the exact text in three languages— one of them is hieroglyphics, the other demotic, and the other ancient Greek. However, lucky for us, these historians were able to read ancient Greek, which made it much easier to know what was written in the other languages. Today, the stone is displayed in the British Museum in London and is available to be seen.

Architecture

When people think about Egypt, one of the first things that comes to mind is the great pyramids. Yes, the great pyramids are an extraordinary example of Ancient Egyptian architecture, but there is a lot more to know about what they built. Egyptians also built temples, monuments, gardens, tombs, and fortresses.

Because there is almost no wood in Egypt due to the existence of the desert, most of the constructions at the time were made from sun-dried bricks that came from the soils of the Nile River. They also used sand and gravel to complement the structures, as well as limestone for decoration.

Art

Arts and crafts were very important in Ancient Egypt. Although they did not have any precious metals such as gold and silver, they had a lot of clay to work with from the Nile, which made it its main type of art for some time. The pottery had a reddish-like color, and the Egyptians mastered its creation. However, they soon started using the clay for other purposes, such as building statues of the pharaohs, of the gods, and even in constructions. When they did these kinds of work, they paid a lot of attention so that everything would be proportional and symmetric, which means that all the sides had to be the same and that one thing was not a lot bigger or smaller than the other so that it didn't look strange.

The Ancient Egyptians also liked to paint. This can be seen in the drawings in the tombs, the palaces, and the temples. They used six colors: red, green, blue, yellow, white, and black. Every color had a meaning and was used to represent specific things, such as blue and green representing plants, the water and the sky, and gold representing the sun. Like the clay work, most of the paintings done by the Egyptians were related to religion and to the kings, who were generally pictured bigger than the other elements because of their importance. This was a general rule—the more important you were, the larger your drawing would be.

Finally, there are the relief carvings, which means you have a wall, for example, and you carve something on it so that a form or an image pops out. The Egyptians used this technique a lot, and it can also be seen in the temples, especially on the walls. Some kings had relief carvings on their walls, representing divinities or rulers. Other things that were carved were stones and ivory tusks.

CHAPTER 4
PHARAOHS

The pharaoh was the ruler of Egypt, known to be both the head of state and the religious leader of the people. A curiosity for you is that the word 'pharaoh' means "great house," but it was soon used as a synonym for the king or queen. Another interesting thing you should know is that although most people refer to all the kings and queens of Egypt as pharaohs, it was only during the New Kingdom that this title was used. To make things easier, we will adopt the popular term 'pharaoh' for all of the rulers of Ancient Egypt.

Ancient Egypt had many famous rulers, both men, and women, out of a total of approximately 300 rulers. They were usually sons, daughters, or declared heirs of the kings who came before, who inherited the throne after their parent's death. During this time, the kings wanted to keep their bloodline clean, so most of the kings married daughters of nobles or princesses. Sometimes, they also married their sisters or half-sisters.

The pharaoh is said to have two jobs—religious leader and head of state. As the religious leader of the people, he was supposed to be the intermediary between the gods and the population, interpreting what the gods wanted and appointing priests to take care of the divinities. As the head of the state, the pharaoh was supposed to rule the country and protect its borders from invaders while invading other countries to look for natural resources, goods, and riches that they did not have in Egypt. It was also the pharaoh's duty to collect taxes, lead the military, and care for the people.

Throughout the history of Ancient Egypt, the name 'pharaoh' gained importance until it reached its peak in the New Kingdom. However, these were also some of the most turbulent times that the Egyptians faced and, therefore, the name then lost its power. It once was a symbol of status and strength, but when the Persians and Alexander the Great invaded the country, it lost most of its status.

In this chapter, you will learn about some of the most famous Egyptian pharaohs. For many of them, very little information is known for many of them because of the destruction of tombs due to war and the lack of historical documents.

Menes (2930 B.C.-2900 B.C.)

King Menes was the first ruler of Ancient Egypt, known to have unified Upper and Lower Egypt. He established the First Dynasty and founded the country's first capital in Memphis. Other names attributed to him are Narmer and Aha, the first being more commonly heard.

Djoser (2686 B.C.-2649 B.C.)

King Djoser reigned during the Third Dynasty, and the most significant accomplishment attributed to him is the construction of the first pyramid—the Step Pyramid.

Khufu (2589 B.C.-2566 B.C.)

The main accomplishment of this king of the Fourth Dynasty was the construction of the Great Pyramid of Giza. The pyramid, which was known to be the tallest structure built by man for almost 4000 years, is still one of Egypt's main touristic points today and was built as the king's stairway to heaven. Little is known about his reign and what he looked like since only one statue of him was recovered. Pieces of others were found inside the constructions he built, but none is enough to give a clear picture.

Hatshepsut (1478 B.C.-1458 B.C.)

Hatshepsut was the second queen to assume control of the country. She is considered a successful ruler, keeping peace and establishing trade routes. She was said to have connections to divinity since she claimed that her mother was visited by the god Amun-Ra during her pregnancy. Although a woman, portraits of Hatshepsut show the image of a woman who dressed like a man and had a male's characteristics, such as a beard and shaved head. She had only one daughter, and once she gained power (which she stole from her stepson), she adopted a more feminine look. Some of her most considerable accomplishments are regarding construction—first of the temple of what would later become known as the Valley of Kings and later the temple of Karnak.

Amenhotep III (1388 B.C.-1351 B.C.)

Amenhotep III did not have much military trouble, as his reign was characterized by being peaceful and economically stable since he took power during one of the most prosperous

EGYPTIAN MYTHOLOGY FOR KIDS

periods in Egypt. One of the main things that were found from his time as a ruler are 200 stone scarabs (stone-carved beetles) that documented part of his reign. He also distributed stone tablets with messages throughout the kingdom, which left good documentation of the time. His temples were not preserved, leaving only two statues of him so that people could have an idea of what he looked like.

Akhenaten (1351 B.C.-1334 B.C.)

Pharaoh Akhenaten was the son of Amenhotep III. He was named Amenhotep IV, but he changed his name once he became king. One of his main characteristics, which differed from most of the Egyptians at the time, was that he was a monotheist, which means he believed in only one god. This god was the sun god Ra and it even led him to move the country's capital from Thebes to Amarna. At the same time, he was not saving any money and ordered that a new capital be built in an inhabited part of Egypt. His wishes for the country almost left it bankrupt, especially due to the radical changes he wanted to make—he wanted it to be a revolution in the country. Yes, maybe he was a little crazy.

This king was almost as known as his wife, Nefertiti, who played an important part when he was the ruler. She supported him during his decisions to change the religion in Egypt and his other plans. Nefertiti is known for a limestone bust made in honor, an object of art that is one of the most copied in the world of those belonging to Ancient Egypt. She is the mother of three of his daughters and the famous King Tutankhamun.

Tutankhamun (1332 B.C.-1323 B.C.)

The most famous pharaoh of Ancient Egypt, King Tutankhamun, was probably close to your age when he became king—he was just 9 or 10 years old. Can you imagine ruling a country while you are a kid? He was famous not because of anything he did but because his tomb was found practically untouched in 1922. Many museums around the world have pieces that were found in his tomb, and you can see them and have a taste of what it was like to be a king in Ancient Egypt. Commonly known as King Tut, he died when he was just 20 years old but denied his father's (Akhenaten) wishes of having a monotheist Egypt and brought back polytheism or the belief in many gods.

The Tomb of Tutankhamun

King Tut's tomb is the only tomb discovered to the present day which was left relatively untouched. It was found in 1922 by a

British archaeologist named Howard Carter in the Valley of the Kings. Although there were signs that the tomb had been raided during Ancient Egyptian times, the main room of the tomb was left untouched. One of the characteristics of the tomb was that it was untidy. Still, historians are unsure if it is because of the robberies or because it had to be finished quickly since the king died at a very young age and the preparations were not ready.

Among the objects found inside the tomb were walking sticks (it is believed that he had a problem with his leg, so he needed help to walk), sculptures of gods, boats, and chariots, among other things. During the emptying of the tomb, over 5000 objects were counted by the archaeologists. Can you believe it? That is a lot! There were so many things inside King Tut's tomb that it took no less than eight years to empty them. Can you imagine having your room filled with so many things that it takes eight years to clean it all up?

In any case, the discovery of this tomb is one of the most important in modern history because it allows us to have a small glimpse of what the pharaoh's tombs looked like originally. Today the room can be visited by only a few people. However, due to the great demand of curious people and tourists who wanted to see what a tomb was like, a copy was made nearby so that the original art did not get ruined and the structure was not compromised with so many visitors. Today, most of the treasures found inside the tomb can be seen in the Cairo Museum in Cairo, Egypt.

Ramses The Great (1279 B.C.-1213 B.C.)

Ramses II, also known as Ramses the Great, was a great king. He was the father of no less than 96 children. Yes, you read that right. He had 96 children! He was also not afraid of spending money, which almost left Egypt without any. He built temples, cities, and monuments, especially since he thought he was a god, so he wanted the whole country to support him through his constructions. He also did some things that weren't very nice—he had slaves and also claimed he created some places that other kings had built.

Cleopatra (51 B.C.-30 B.C.)

Raise your hand if you have ever heard about Egypt's most famous queen: Cleopatra. If you haven't, no worries: I will tell you more about her. She was the last pharaoh of Ancient Egypt and is very famous. She even had many movies made about her and books written about her life. Cool, huh? Egyptologists claim that she was beautiful, had a calm voice, and spoke many languages. However, since there are so many stories about her, people have a hard time telling apart what is the truth and what is a myth.

She was born in Greece, and one of the main things she did was bring peace to Egypt. She is also known for having romantic relationships and children with two Romans, the ruler Julius Caesar and the general Marc Anthony, when the Romans invaded Egypt.

A curiosity about Cleopatra is that her tomb was never found. Archeologists keep looking for it to learn more about the famous Egyptian queen. Still, other than rumors, nothing has been found so far.

CHAPTER 5
GODS AND GODDESSES

Ancient Egypt's population was polytheist, meaning they worshiped more than one god. Egyptians believed that there was a god that represented different things in their life, such as the sun, the air, and death. Egyptologists have identified over 1500 deities, which is another name for gods, but there are many more that remain unidentified in the Egyptian pantheon. It is believed that the number can be well over 2000. Can you imagine? Two thousand gods to worship! How did they keep track of it all? I guess that remains a mystery.

Although Egyptians had temples for worshiping these gods, these were controlled by the priests named by the pharaohs and were not accessible to the public. Yes, you read it right.

The temples were built for the gods but, unlike today, people could not go inside them. What happened was that during the specific day dedicated to the god, they would be brought out from the temple so that the people could celebrate them. Then they would be taken back inside until the next festival.

The temples were built to please the gods, as the people would do anything to be on their good side. This also means making offerings to them and holding festivals in their honor. The priests treated the statues, or representation of the gods as if they were real people, can you believe it? They would give their statues food and water, clothe them, decorate them with jewelry, and do their makeup.

When studying the Egyptian divinities, it is possible to see that they have animal characteristics or are represented by animals most of the time. It is believed that these gods were initially symbolized by animals but later, with the development of the culture, changed to the representation of humans with an animal head. Another curious fact is that some of the gods who are portrayed as humans are drawn with the thing they represent on top of their heads. For example, the god of the sun has a sun on top of his head. Due to the size of the Egyptian kingdom, it was not unusual for two gods to represent the same thing in different regions, leading to one shadowing the other on some occasions.

Because of the large number of worshiped gods (remember, over 2000!), their importance was constantly changing due to the season or a certain event. It was also common for one god to absorb characteristics of another throughout time or for two gods to become one, such as the example of Amun-Ra. Here are a few of the main Egyptian gods and their characteristics.

Nut and Geb

The Egyptians believed that all of the gods descended from the same family, which in this case were Nut, the sky goddess, and Geb, the god of the Earth. These gods were married, and Nut, who was the mother, gave birth to the five original gods: Osiris, Isis, Set, Nephthys, and Horus, the Elder. Nut is usually represented in human form, and it is said that each of her limbs represents a cardinal point—north, south, east, and west. Since she was the goddess of the sky, she is generally found in drawings on the ceilings of the tombs. Geb is associated with fertility and is considered to be the father of snakes. Myths in Ancient Egypt said that his laugh caused the earthquakes.

Osiris

Osiris was the god of the underworld, who symbolized death, resurrection, and the cycle of the Nile floods, which are associated with agricultural fertility. He was married to his sister Isis, who brought him back to life after being killed by his brother, Set. He is considered one of the most powerful gods, and because of that, the Egyptians wanted to be buried near his temple. He is usually portrayed as a mummy or as having green-blue skin, a color that is associated with the dead. He is the lord of death and, in the Egyptian Book of the Dead, he is the judge of those who comes into the afterlife.

Isis

Isis is considered one of the most important goddesses in Egyptian culture and represents a mother and wife's virtues. This is because of her dedication to resurrecting her husband. She is also the mother of Horus, who she had with Osiris. Isis is associated with every aspect of human life and became a powerful goddess represented with a throne on her head in drawings. She is also depicted breastfeeding Horus, which some scholars consider to be the inspiration for pictures of Mary feeding Jesus. Her most famous temple is located in Philae, and she is commonly associated with the Greek goddess Aphrodite. She was one of the last goddesses to be worshiped when the Romans invaded Egypt.

Horus

Horus was the son of Isis and Osiris and was conceived to get revenge on his uncle, Set, for his father's death. He is generally depicted as a falcon or a man with a falcon's head. His most known symbol is the Eye of Horus since one of his eyes represented the sun and the other the moon. Myths say that during his battle with Set, which he won, he lost one eye, the one that represented the moon, which is the reason for the moon's phases.

Set

Set is the god of chaos, violence, deserts, and storms, which he is said to bring to the valley of the Nile. He is the brother and killer of Osiris but is not considered to be evil. According to Egyptian myth, he is a balance to the goodness in all of the other gods. He is generally pictured as a beast with hooves and a forked tail.

Nephthys

Nephthys is the twin sister of Isis and the wife of Set. Although she did not carry a negative connotation, she is considered the funerary goddess and the darkness to Isis' light. She is the Egyptian funerary goddess, mostly believed because she helped her sister set up Set for battle after the murder of Osiris, which she didn't agree with. She is generally represented with a basket on her head and is the mother of Anubis.

Anubis

Anubis is the Egyptian god who cared for the dead and was the god of the underworld before Osiris. He was said to guide the souls through the Hall of the Truth before they were judged by Osiris in the afterlife. He is represented as a jackal or a human with the head of a jackal carrying a staff. Historians believe that the representation of the god as a jackal is because these dogs would surround dead bodies when they were not buried.

Ptah, Sekhmet and Nefertem

This family of father, mother and son was a divine trinity worshiped in Memphis. Ptah appears in the historic drawings during the First Dynastic Period. He is said to be the creator of the universe and the lord of truth, and an early fertility god. He is the patron of the craftsman and the architects since it was believed that he designed the earth's shape. His wife, Sekhmet, is represented as a woman with the head of a lion. She is the goddess of destruction and healing and the patron of the Egyptian military. Some myths say that she is also the daughter of Ra. The son of the couple, Nefertem, is the god of perfume and sweet aromas. He is also considered the god of rebirth and transformation on some occasions.

Hathor

Hathor is an Egyptian goddess represented by a cow or a woman with the head of a cow with horns and sun in the middle. She was believed to protect women during childbirth and was the goddess of music, dancing, inspiration, drunkenness, celebration, and love. Most of the temples built in her honor are located on the west of the Nile River, and the most famous one is located in Dendara. Her characteristics are believed to later have been absorbed by Isis or, in some other stories, she is a later incarnation of Sekhmet. In some stories, she is the daughter of Ra and, in others, the wife of Horus. She was also associated with the Greek goddess Aphrodite.

Bastet

Bastet is a goddess with the form of a cat or a woman with a cat's head. She was associated with the Greek goddess Artemis, divine hunter and goddess of the moon. She is believed to be the daughter of Ra. As the cat was considered a sacred animal in Ancient Egypt, many Egyptians carried a talisman with her in cat form as a sign of good luck and protection.

Heka

One of the oldest gods in Ancient Egypt, Heka was the god of magic and medicine and the guiding force of the universe. He is generally drawn as a man carrying a staff and a knife. He is the patron of doctors due to his healing powers. He is associated by the Greeks with the god Hermes.

Serket

Although Serket is not one of the most famous goddesses, she is known to the public because there was an enormous statue of her made of gold in the tomb of the pharaoh Tutankhamun. She is a funerary and protective goddess who protects children in particular. She was usually invoked for her healing powers.

Thoth and Seshat

Thoth and Seshat were a divine couple associated with writing. Thoth was considered the god of wisdom and writing, having invented the language and the hieroglyphic script, serving as a scribe to the other gods. Due to this, he is the patron of libraries and scribes. He also has magical powers and is the holder of secrets. He was especially worshiped in the Predynastic Period and is considered the last man to rule Egypt and the son of Ra. He is drawn as a baboon or the man with the head of an ibis. Seshat, his wife, or sometimes daughter, is the goddess of writing, notations, measurements, and books. She is mentioned for the first time in the Second Dynasty, and it is said that pharaohs called her when they wanted to properly build their temples. There is no knowledge that Seshat had a temple of her own. She is generally depicted as a woman with leopard skin who has a robe covering her. She is also shown as a woman with a headband holding a stick with a star on top.

Ra, Amun, and Amun-Ra

Before becoming the powerful and most known Egyptian god Amun-Ra, the god was, in fact, two different gods: Amun and Ra. Ra is a god associated with the sun, represented by a human body and the head of a hawk. He used to be the sun-god of Heliopolis and became very popular in the fifth dynasty. Ra is said to drive his sun barge daily across the sky and dive into the afterworld by night, where he faces Apep, the serpent, who threatens him every day. He is one of the most long-lasting gods and is characterized by a sun-disk resting on his head. Amun was also a god of national importance, but he is said to have his origins in Thebes as the sun god. He is represented as a man wearing a crown with two plumes. These two gods merged and became the most powerful god in Egypt—Amun-Ra, the god of sun and air and the King of all the gods.

CHAPTER 6
DEATH AND THE AFTERLIFE

Before you start this chapter, let me tell you that I know talking about death can be uncomfortable and even scary. However, this was a major aspect of the life and beliefs of the Egyptians, so we need to talk about it so you can understand it better. But don't worry. There will be nothing scary about it, just some stories and practices of how they dealt with death and the afterlife. For example, did you know that the pharaohs used to have their tombs filled with offerings to have a comfortable afterlife? See, there is nothing bad about it. It is just people caring for their loved ones who passed away.

However, if you get scared or upset, don't worry. Remember that this is just a book that talks about things that happened a long, long time ago. These ideas were common at the time and part of their culture. They even built temples and magnificent tombs for the afterlife filled with drawings and decorations. So be brave, hang on and come see some of the beautiful things the Egyptians did for those who died.

Death

Death was so close to Ancient Egyptian culture that many of their symbols are related to death. Mummies? Related to death. Pyramids? Related to death. Tomb drawings and offerings? Related to death. Well, I guess you get the picture of how much the Egyptians related their life to eventual death. Their culture is considered one of the richest when talking about the subject.

They believed in life after death, so, to the people in Ancient Egypt, death was just a temporary passing. They had many rituals they performed when a loved one passed away, including building tombs, making sarcophagi and coffins, embalming and mummifying the bodies and animals, and leaving them with enough possessions to be used in the afterlife. Death was so important to the Egyptians that it was almost considered a celebration when they would honor the life of the person who passed away. They had the knowledge that death would come to everyone at one point or another.

Life in the old ages was short for many reasons. This affected not only the general population but also nobles and kings. Because people often died young in Ancient Egypt, the rituals surrounding the death were popular. The body had to be kept intact if the person's spirit came black to claim it to use in the afterlife, which is why they developed the mummification technique.

The Afterlife

The Egyptians made offerings to the gods and left objects, food, drink, and other objects in the tomb for those who died since they believed that after death, the spirit would depart the body, but only temporarily. In the afterlife, a soul would go to the underworld to be judged by Osiris. However, before reaching the judge and lord of the dead, the soul needed to go through several gates before reaching eternal joy. They would go through the Hall of Truth in the company of Anubis before reaching the final judgment.

When the soul got to Osiris, it would be decided if it would go to heaven, called the Field of Reeds, or stay in the darkness.

The most common belief is that the person had the same experience that they used to have while living in the afterlife. Another important thing is that most Egyptians weren't interested in moving on. They believed that everything they needed was in their home, in their land, so they just expected everything to be the same.

These are some of the most common versions of the afterlife, but many kept changing through time. There is also the story about the 42 confessions when a soul would confess their sins in front of the gods, who would judge them and decide if they should go to the Field of Reeds by a magical boat or not. The dead would serve Ra in his daily travels through the sky in another version. This means that not only did they have a very rich culture, but also a very good imagination for storytelling.

Book of the Dead

The Book of the Dead was a book that contained spells that were used when a person died. It was used during most of the period of Ancient Egypt, although it kept changing and improving through time. Even though it is called "the book" of the dead, it had many different copies and no two were the same: Printing came only a long time afterward, so these books were written by hand. The books had illustrations and writing, and because of the difficulty, the high level of personalization, and the elaborate means to make them, only people with a lot of money could afford these writings.

The book was usually buried with the person so that they could use it in case they needed to use the spells. The underworld was a dangerous place, with traps, threats, dangerous animals, and threatening souls. The Book of the Dead also instructed the soul on how to act on these occasions, as if it were a manual on what the person should expect at every stage of the afterlife. This book has become popular recently, with many movies and books making reference to it. You have probably seen it in films such as Harry Potter, the Mummy, or others that deal with magic or Egyptian culture.

Spell 125

If there was one constant in The Book of the Dead, it was spell 125. A copy of this specific spell was found in all of the versions studied by historians. Let's find out what made it so special.

Spell 125 talks about the procedure of weighing the heart, where the gods put the person's heart on a scale to determine if they would go to paradise or not. To pass the test, the person had to know exactly what to say to the gods so that the answer would be positive. The heart was weighed after the individual confessed to the 42 sins and, if it weighed less than the feather of the truth, the person could move on. The spell begins by stating exactly what should be said to Osiris and describes the different situations.

Mummies

Have you ever heard about a creature called a mummy? You have? On Halloween, right? Well, did you know that the Egyptians were responsible for the first mummies ever? And very much like the image we usually have of them, they did, in fact, have their body wrapped. But let's not get ahead of ourselves. Let's start from the beginning, and I will tell you everything there is to know about mummies. Ready?

When a person died in Ancient Egypt, their body went through a process called embalming. This consisted of removing the moisture from the body and leaving it completely dry so that it would not decay quickly. They wanted the body to be preserved so that the soul could return to it in the afterlife and use it if necessary. So, it was important to keep as many good physical traits as possible. This process was so efficient that even today, almost 4000 years later, we can know what the people at that time looked like because their bodies are so well-preserved. This process was so good and efficient that it was used throughout most of Egyptian history and influenced how we put our loved ones to rest today.

Even though it was a good process, it was a really long and unpleasant one, so no details! The mummification took about 70 days to be completed. Can you imagine? Seventy days! That is a little more than two months! The priests were responsible for taking care of the bodies, and they wrapped the body with hundreds of meters of cloth. However, while wrapping the mummy, they would put amulets in between the wraps and write prayers and magical words on the wrappings, all for the good passage of the person who had died.

After the mummy was ready, it was placed inside a tomb, which generally was built long before the person had died, especially if they were a noble or a king or queen. Inside the tomb would be the mummy and a series of offerings for them to use in the afterlife. Sometimes, even their mummified pets were there. Other things that were also in the tomb were food, water, furniture, clothes, scrolls of papyrus, drawings, statues, and pottery. After all of this was prepared, they were ready for the funeral.

Mortuary Temples

Once the pharaohs stopped building pyramids to use as funeral homes for their bodies, they started giving more importance to the mortuary temples. During the pyramid era, they were an attachment to the construction and served as a place to deposit the offerings and house the chapel. These grandiose temples were more common during the new kingdom, where every new ruler or spouse built their own part to be put to rest. Today, the most famous ones are the Temple of Hatshepsut, the Valley of Kings, and the Valley of Queens.

The Temple of Hatshepsut

As we have seen earlier, Hatshepsut was one of Egypt's most famous pharaohs. She determined that her mortuary temple be built as soon as she took power, and she wanted it to be grand. It was supposed to tell the story of her life and her reign and be above any other temple in greatness and beauty. The temple has two ramps, two floors, and many large obelisks. Everything inside the temple was grand and luxurious: pools, sphinxes, statues, art, and much more. It is not only a temple but a sanctuary that includes gardens and memorials as well.

Valley of the Kings

The Valley of Kings is one of Egypt's most visited tourist attractions. The Valley of the Kings is located to the west of the Nile River in the region of Upper Egypt. It was the burial site for almost all the pharaohs of the last dynasties, which added up to more or less 70 kings. The region was chosen because it was in a lonely valley, and the pharaohs believed that their burial site would be protected if fewer people had access to them. Along with the kings, some queens and members of the military are also buried in the complex, as well as the children of some of the rulers. All of the tombs are different in design, as each king built theirs as they saw fit and to their taste. However, they do have some things in common, such as tomb art and sculptures engraved on the walls. It was in this complex that, in 1922, the tomb of the young and famous pharaoh Tutankhamun was found by archaeologists.

Valley of the Queens

The Valley of the Queens, similar to the Valley of the Kings, is a structure also located to the west of the Nile, and it is where the queens were buried after their death. It is located near the Valley of the Kings and even the ruler's children were buried there with their mothers. Although it is composed of 75 tombs, only four are open to the public, including that of Nefertari, the favorite wife of Ramses, the Great. The tomb is colorful, with decorated walls, many corridors, and drawings of the stars on the ceiling.

CHAPTER 7
PYRAMIDS

One of the most iconic treasures known today in Ancient Egypt is the pyramids. Have you ever heard of them? They attract millions of tourists every year who wish to enter them to see and learn a little about what happened during that time. Like I have said before, the first pyramid was built during the Third Dynasty, but it was during the Old Kingdom that most of them were constructed. Once a pharaoh took power, the first thing he would do was to instruct that a new pyramid be built so that it could be ready when he died. Even though most people only know of the three pyramids of Giza, Egypt has around 140 structures of this kind spread across its territory, although mainly to the west of the Nile River.

Although they are the most recognized architecture throughout the country, the pyramid was part of a larger complex that involved gardens, temples, and other constructions. They were initially built only for the pharaohs, but later nobles and members of the higher Egyptian society began building them too. The main objective of the pyramid was to protect and provide for the king's soul in the afterlife and, for this reason, most of them had treasures, food, and other goods stored in them. Historians believe that the pyramids were built in the direction of the sky to help the pharaoh's soul go up to the heavens.

The first known architect of pyramids is Imhotep, a priest during Djoser's reign. Before using pyramids as tombs, the Egyptians used a structure called the mastabas, which were mounds with an angled shape. Imhotep used his creativity to design a building with one mastaba on top of the other. Additionally, tunnels, passages, and rooms were added under the structure to store the offerings to the king or queen, to place his body after death, and even bury other people who were close relatives or servants for the afterlife.

Soon the tombs started having drawings and scripts of the leader's reign and stories and offerings for the gods. These are the earliest registries of Egyptian culture, known as tomb art, which include descriptions of daily life in Egypt, customs, and other rituals carried by them. The inscriptions and art in the Egyptian tombs allowed researchers to better understand the life of these people as well as have a better understanding of their grammar and language.

It is important to say that, while the pyramids remain to be grand structures today, accounts of Egyptologists say that they were even more important when they were built. Today, most of them have gone through a lot of deterioration because they were not properly maintained, which led to the loss of some of their characteristics. Furthermore, robberies and vandalism of the constructions have left the pyramids with little of their original content, such as the remains of the pharaohs, the offerings they had, and the treasures they contained. Finally, it is important to note that even though 138 pyramids are accounted for, a large portion of them was left unfinished, possibly due to the short reign of the kings who ordered them.

Next, you will see, in chronological order of construction, some of the most iconic pyramids which can be found in Egypt. The best part of all is that if you get really curious and decide that you want to see them up close and for real, you can, since most of them are open for visitation.

Step Pyramid

The Step Pyramid was the first structure of its kind built in Egypt. It was built during the Old Kingdom for King Djoser and is composed of six layers. It is 60 meters high and has around five kilometers of tunnels inside. It was named the Step Pyramid because its design resembles steps.

Buried Pyramid

Since this pyramid was not finished, there is little to no information about it. It is believed to have been built under the order of King Djoser's successor and designed by Imhotep as well. However, stories say that the ruler Sekhemkhet Djoserty died before the construction could be completed and, therefore, it was never finished.

Pyramid of Meidum

The pyramid of Meidum, unlike the ones built before it, was the first pyramid to have straight sides instead of a step-like structure. Its original height is believed to be a little over 90 meters and, contrary to the other pyramids, it was built on top of the sand, not stone, which compromised its structure and led to the collapse of a part of it, although another reason could be that it was also left unfinished.

Bent Pyramid

With a height of 105 meters, the bent pyramid was built for the ruler Sneferu in Dashur and has a unique architecture compared to the other pyramids—it appears to be bent! This is because the structure of the building had to be changed during its construction because it began to collapse and crack, scaring the constructors into modifying it before it became completely ruined. This pyramid is today open for visitors to enter and it is possible to see the tunnels and the burial rooms inside.

Red Pyramid

The red pyramid has this name because... Yes! It has this name due to the color of its bricks, which are red. This pyramid was also built by king Sneferu after the construction of the bent pyramid. It is the third-largest structure of the kind in Egypt, only after two of the great pyramids in Giza. This pyramid is considered the first smooth-sided pyramid which was built successfully and is open for visitors. One curiosity about this pyramid, as well as for most of the other pyramids, is that it wasn't originally red, but rather covered with a white layer of limestone so that it would shine. However, tomb raiders and thieves have stolen these parts and now almost none of the structures have them.

The Pyramids of Giza

The complex of the pyramids of Giza is the most known in Egypt since they are the first and second tallest structures of the kind. Like the other pyramids, they have formal names, in order of construction and size, Khufu, Khafre, and Menkaure, names of the kings who had them built. Khufu, the tallest of the pyramids, had an original height of 147 meters; Khafre had an original height of 143 meters, and Menakure had an original height of 65 meters. The pyramids in this complex have many tunnels and burial chambers and are also available for public visitation. However, most of the goods buried with the kings are missing since they have been the object of raids and thefts over the years. The Great Pyramid of Giza is considered one of the Seven Wonders of the world due to its importance.

Also, near the pyramids rests another iconic Egyptian construction, the Sphinx. It is said to have been built to protect the pyramids and the bodies of the kings laid in them. It is 73 meters long and 20 meters high and is the sculpture of a lion with a human head, which supposedly belongs to King Khafre. As you will have noticed, the nose in the face of the Sphinx is missing, and how that happened is unknown. What Egyptologists do know is that the structure has deteriorated over the years and that most of its original paintings and characteristics are gone. Some say that during Napoleon's invasion of Egypt, the nose was shot off with a cannon, but that cannot be verified.

Pyramid of Sahure

This pyramid, although small (it was only 47 meters tall), is important because it represents another change in the way that pyramids were built. In this case, the structure had a tunnel that connected it to all of the other adjourning constructions: mortuary, temple, and valley temple. It was built during the Fifth Dynasty and set the standard for the next pyramids that were built.

Pyramid of Unas

Although the Pyramid of Unas is a relatively small pyramid built by king Unas, the last ruler of the Fifth Dynasty, it is important because it was the first of its kind to have tomb texts on them. It contained spells for the pharaoh's afterlife, and the story of his kingdom, among other information. Although the pyramid is open for tourist visitation, most of its external structure has significantly deteriorated. The inside, however, is mostly intact and allows the visitor insight into what the tombs used to be like.

CHAPTER 8
TECHNOLOGY AND
INVENTIONS

What would you say if I told you that many of the things we use today were invented by the Ancient Egyptians? I know, it sounds crazy, but did you know that they were the ones who invented items such as the toothbrush and toothpaste and the police? Yes, that police. The Ancient Egyptians were the first ones to have police officers; plus, they even used dogs like we do today! Let's take a look at other inventions made by them that we still use in daily life.

Medical Tools

Can you imagine what it was like if you got sick in Ancient Egypt and had to go to the doctor? Well, you wouldn't need to worry because the doctors in Egypt had some of the most advanced knowledge in the medical field. Some documents describe injuries, treatments, and diagnostics in detail, especially for the upper part of the body. The treatments included bandages and other materials we commonly see today, including some used for surgery.

Toothpaste and Toothbrush

Like I said before, it was in Ancient Egypt that the first form of toothpaste and toothbrush was invented. It may sound a little disgusting, but the recipe for toothpaste was ox hooves, ashes, burnt eggshells, and pumice. Can you imagine the taste? Another recipe, uncovered in a papyrus found in a tomb, probably tasted less yucky. It was made of rock salt, mint, dried iris flower, and pepper grains. Believe it or not, the products also came with advertisements—they claimed that this was the recipe for a powder that would leave your teeth white!

But why would they invent these things? Well, first of all, there were a lot of dental problems in Ancient Egypt; all these pictures that we see of the kings with perfect teeth are probably not true. Second, since Egypt is in the desert, a lot of sand used to get mixed with the food, so they wanted something to get it off their mouths after they ate. This is because if the sand was left in the mouth, it would wear down their teeth to their roots, exposing the pulp and making it easier to get an infection.

Breath Mints

Still, about dentistry, the Ancient Egyptians were also the first ones to use something that is very common today, and you can buy it in any gas station store: breath mints! Because of their poor dental health, their breath was probably also not the best. Therefore, why not invent something that would make it more pleasant to get near a person to hear them speak? So, they did exactly that. Historians believe that these mints were a candy-shaped mixture of frankincense, myrrh, and cinnamon boiled with honey.

Papyrus and Ink

Even though the paper was only invented by the Chinese much later, the Egyptians found a good alternative to write their scrolls and texts: papyrus. Using fibers from the plant that was grown on the banks of the Nile, they discovered that it could be used for writing. However, what were they going to write with? Well, with ink-black ink, specifically. Black ink was a mixture of vegetable gum, soot, and beeswax. As time passed, they discovered that they could substitute the soot for other elements in order to make different colors.

Cosmetics

One thing that the pictures drawn of Ancient Egypt will tell us, is that the Egyptians took care of and worried about their appearance. Maybe because this was so important to them, they invented some things that are very common today: eye makeup, perfume, deodorant, nail polish, and hand mirrors.

The hand mirrors can be seen in several drawings from the time, with men and women alike holding the object. Mirrors were generally sculpted and decorated. The quantity of decoration would tell if the person was a noble or someone from the middle class.

There is something that stands out in every drawing, even those we see today—the black makeup around the eyes. This black eye makeup was created by mixing soot with a mineral called galena, generating a black ointment named kohl, which is still used today. The more noble the person was, the more makeup they wore, especially around the eyes. But the eyeliner was not only used for beauty—but they also believed it could cure diseases in the eyes and protect them from the evil eye.

Haircuts, Wigs, and Shaving

While we are still talking about beauty and how it was important for the Egyptians, let's also talk about how they were the first to wear wigs and have a different shave. Well, first, you need to know that it was very common at the time for both men and women to shave their heads because of lice. Yes, it sounds disgusting, and it is, so they would have no hair at all to avoid this problem. However, a woman with a shaved head was not attractive, so they developed the use of wigs so that it would seem that the woman had hair. But hey, they were not only for the ladies; men also wore them, in the most varied shapes and sizes.

In order to cut their hair and beards, the Ancient Egyptians invented the barber profession, as well as the tools that they would use, such as razors. Since being shaved meant that the person was noble and fashionable while having hair meant that they were poor, everyone wanted to look hairless. But not really hairless, only without their original hair, since they would use sheep wool to make fake beards and wear them around town.

Calendar

You might be surprised to hear that the first calendar resembling what we have today was invented in Ancient Egypt. Invented initially by the Sumerians, the calendar was improved and perfected by the Egyptians. Although we use them today to remember special dates and birthdays, of course, the Egyptians used them to track the floods of the Nile. Much similar to our present-day calendar, theirs was divided into 12 months of 30 days each and five additional festive days in honor of the gods at the end of the year, adding to a total of—you guessed it!—365 days. However, we cannot forget that we have a leap year every four years, so although it was mostly correct, it still lacked some information that we have today until one additional day was added every four years.

Clocks

Since we are talking about time, it is important to say that the first clock was invented in Ancient Egypt. But they were not like the clocks we have today. Rather, they were sun clocks. They used the obelisks they built as an indicator of time according to the shadow that was projected by the construction. They could determine time with a lot of precision, including what was a short day (during winter) and what was a long day (during summer).

Bowling

If you like to go bowling, you must be very thankful to the Egyptians. A game similar to the one we have today was played by them more or less at the time that the Romans invaded the country. Archaeologists have found lanes with a square in the middle and balls of different sizes in their excavations. The game was to try to make the balls reach the square in the middle, while also interrupting the path of the ball of your opponents.

Door Lock

If you are at home right now, look at your door. You see a door, a knob, and a keyhole, right? Well, let me just say that you have got the Egyptians to thank for that: They were the inventors of the door lock which keeps you safe at home at night. However, although they were mostly safe, they were not very practical as they were very big, reaching up to half a meter in length.

Police

Since we are talking about security, let's talk about something that I am almost sure you would not imagine—the police force was created by the Ancient Egyptians. In early Ancient Egyptian times, the local officials kept order in the cities with private police forces but, after a while, it became more centralized. They even used dogs, much like we do today. No one was above the law and punishments of the most varied kind were given to those who committed an infraction.

Tools

The people in Ancient Egypt were very innovative and good tool makers. For example, the first ox plow used in agriculture was invented by them. They also invented canals, reservoirs, and irrigation systems to use the water of the Nile on their farms. Finally, to enable them to build their constructions, the Egyptians developed the lever, in order to facilitate transporting materials.

CHAPTER 9
STORIES AND MYTHS

Like most ancient cultures, the Egyptians had many myths regarding their gods. Some of them were heroes, others were villains. There were myths and stories about wars and about the creation of the earth. Some gods went to war, others stayed with their families. All of these were myths or stories invented by the Egyptian people about the beloved gods and goddesses they worshiped.

However, the Egyptians didn't only have myths about gods and goddesses. They also had tales that told how the pharaoh was deceived or a love story between him and another girl. In this chapter, I will tell you some of the most popular myths from Ancient Egypt and you can choose the one you like the most. Oh, Yes! Keep your eyes open in this chapter for a very special surprise—you just might recognize one of the tales as a popular one told today!

The Myth of Creation

As we have seen in previous chapters, Ra was one of the most powerful gods in Ancient Egypt. Throughout time, people began attributing more and more powers to him. One claim was that Ra was responsible for creating all the gods of the Earth. It was also said that every day, the god would make a journey across the sky in the form of the sun, and, at night, he would go to the underworld and fight with Apep, the serpent. When there was an eclipse or no sun, the Egyptians would say that it was because Ra had lost the fight and was swallowed by Apep.

Another story stated that there was an egg that named all living beings on the Earth and, once that was done, it became a man who was the first Pharaoh of Egypt. This man was said to be Ra and, because of this, the kings claimed that they were the Sons of Ra, since they were from a direct line from the god and, thus, had the right to the throne.

The Myth of Osiris and Isis

Isis and Osiris were two of the five children of Nut, and even though they were brother and sister, they were also married. Because Osiris was Nut and Geb's oldest son, he soon became the king, and boy was he loved. Since everyone adored Osiris, his brother, Set, became jealous and decided that he would kill him. When he did, he spread Osiris' pieces all over Egypt.

Isis, upset because her husband had died, decided to use her powers to bring back her husband to life. She traveled across Egypt picking up Osiris' pieces and resurrected him by using a magic spell. After he was reborn, the couple magically had a child they named Horus. However, even though he was living again, Osiris wasn't allowed to go back to the world of the living and went to the underworld to be their ruler and judge.

Isis and the Seven Scorpions

The tale of Isis and the seven scorpions was a very famous myth in Ancient Egypt. It tells the story of how Isis, after the death of Osiris, tried to hide from Set, but he found her anyway. However, Isis was pregnant, and Thoth thought that she would be in danger if Set found out, so he ran to save her. In order for Set not to find her, she was hidden by seven scorpions who promised to protect Isis and her son.

Isis then used her magic to change her form and adopted one of the poor women. During her travel, she decided to stop at the house of a rich woman and ask for some food and a place to rest. However, this woman was very mean and, when she saw the beggar, shut the door in her face. The scorpions were very angry, but Isis just continued to walk and was sheltered in the house of a poor fisher girl, who gave her food and a place to stay for the night.

The scorpions, however, were not going to forget what the rich woman did to Isis and told Serket, who was the one who sent them as the goddess' bodyguards. She instructed one of the scorpions to sting the rich woman's son. He did and the boy almost died. The mother cried for help, and it was Isis who saw and took pity on her, thus saving the boy and forgiving the woman.

The Myth of Horus and Set

As you know, Horus was the child of Osiris and Isis. He grew up to be a very brave man and decided that he would get revenge on his uncle, Set, for murdering his father. He did this by challenging Set to the throne since he had become the ruler after Osiris' death. Their battle took many years and it

EGYPTIAN MYTHOLOGY FOR KIDS

involved magic and contests. In the beginning, Set won, because he used tricks and did not play fair.

However, Horus' mother Isis, decided to help her son and set a trap for her brother. When she caught him, she eventually let him go, which made her son and the other gods very angry. Finally, they had the last contest, which was a boat race that Horus won. Set was so very angry that he had lost that he changed his form and became a hippopotamus that destroyed Horus' boat. Of course, because of this, they started fighting again, after all, no one likes to be attacked.

In this last battle, the gods declared that it was a tie, but neither of the men was happy with this result. Therefore, they decided to ask Osiris, who decided in favor of his son, who took his place on the throne.

The Battle of Pelusium

Bastet was the beloved cat-goddess of the Egyptians. However, because their enemies knew of this adoration, they used it to their advantage to win wars. In 525 B.C., in the last battle which the Persians had to conquer Egypt, they used a trick to win.

Knowing about the devotion of the Egyptians to their gods who were represented by animals, especially Bastet, the commander painted images of cats on their shields. He also brought all of the animals that he could find to place on the front line of the battle. No need to say that these animals were dogs, cats, sheep, and ibises, any animal that they knew represented Egyptian gods.

This battle, known as the Battle of Pelusium, was rather curious: The Egyptians lost because they were scared to make their gods and goddesses angry by attacking their images, so they surrendered.

The Myth of Hathor

As you have seen in the chapter about gods and goddesses, Sekhmet was the goddess of love, music, beauty, and more. She was Ra's daughter and represented many good things in the world. However, she also had a bad side to her: She punished people in the name of Ra when they were wicked. One time, Ra was tired of humanity and decided that he was going to destroy them. He asked Sekhmet to do it, but neither he nor the other gods were ready for all the trouble and havoc she would bring.

He tried calling her back but she wouldn't listen to him—she was unstoppable. He then decided to trick her and made large amounts of beer mixed with blood so she would be attracted by the smell. Since she was tired, bored, and thirsty from killing mankind, she decided to drink the beer, but it had magic and she fell into a deep sleep, unable to continue with the destruction. When she woke up, she woke up as Hathor, a benevolent goddess who represented only good things.

The Myth of Anubis

Anubis, who was the guardian of the underworld, was also a protector of tombs. Ancient Egyptians used to tell a story that when a person died, they went to the underworld to be judged by Osiris, and Anubis was there to receive them. He would weigh the person's heart on the Scale of Truth against a feather. If the heart weighed more, the soul would be eaten by a demon: If the heart weighed less, the soul would be allowed to go into the underworld.

The Book of Thoth

A long time ago, there was a prince called Setna, son of Rameses the Great. Setna liked to study a lot and was happy when people left him alone to do so. He knew how to read and write hieroglyphics, and he also knew magic, which he had learned from what he studied. One day, while reading a book, he discovered that a human had read the Book of Thoth and gained incredible magical powers with it, and he decided he would do anything to gain that knowledge.

He left with his two brothers in search of the tomb in which the Book of Thoth was hidden and eventually found it. Guarding the book were two ghosts, who warned Setna not to take the book, as it would bring him trouble. The spirits told him about the challenges faced by Nefrekeptah to find the Book of Thoth—he had recovered the book after a lot of trouble and gained the wisdom of the spells. The Book of Thoth was said to be the most powerful book in all of Egypt. It had all the knowledge of the gods, and the pharaohs were constantly trying to get a hold of it and were never able to. Thoth hid the book in many boxes and placed it on the floor of the Nile, where many serpents guarded it.

However, Nefrekeptah suffered a great loss when he could not save the life of his son and his wife during the journey back home in the Nile, even though he had all the spells from the Book of Thoth. In spite of hearing the warnings, Setna decided that he wanted the book and said he would take it by force, which did not please either the ghosts nor the soul of

Nefrekeptah, who came back to life and said that, in order to have it, he must win it in a competition.

They played a game where every time Setna lost, he sank deeper into the ground. He then asked his brother to bring an amulet to save him and, when he was about to sink to the ground, the amulet was placed on his head. He got up fast and snatched the book away from Nefrekeptah. Although the ghosts guarding the book were scared that he lost his power, he claimed that Setna would bring back the book and beg for forgiveness.

Setna read the book and took it everywhere with him. One day, while he was outside a temple, he saw a girl and fell madly in love with her, which even made him forget the Book of Thoth. He was betrayed by her after she made him kill his children and make his wife a beggar, at the promise of marriage and children. When he woke up, he realized that it was only a dream, the result of a spell cast on him. Once the spell was broken, he found himself naked in the street, being made fun of. After a man gave him a cloak, he went back home and found that it was all a dream.

When he realized this meant that he had to give back the book, as the pharaoh had previously advised him to do, he was scared and thought to beg Neferkaptah for his forgiveness. He did exactly that, but the man was not willing to forgive Setna unless he brought the bodies of his child and wife back to his temple to lay with him. If he did not do as asked, the dream would come true. Setna obeyed and immediately set to look out for the bodies, but did not find them.

Soon a man told him that he knew where the bodies were and Setna found them, taking them back to the tomb. After he left, he said a spell that closed the door of the tomb forever, so that no one would find it.

The Girl With the Rose Red Slippers

This myth is an interesting one and it might remind you of a modern story that you most certainly have already heard. Let's see if you recognize it.

There once was a Greek girl named Rhodopis, who was kidnapped by pirates and sold as a slave in Egypt. She had light hair and pale skin, had a kind heart, and knew how to dance very well. Because of this, she was bought by a man who only showed her kindness, giving her beautiful gifts, including a pair of rose-red slippers so that she could dance. She was planning to use the slippers for a festival that the Pharaoh was going to have but all of the other slaves, envious of the treatment that she had from the master, gave her a lot of work so that she couldn't attend.

Tired of working, she took off her slippers for a few minutes to rest, but an eagle passed by, caught one of them, and flew away. Interestingly enough, the eagle took the slipper and dropped it into Pharaoh Amasis' lap, who decided he wanted to meet the owner of the slipper. It just so happens that this eagle is Horus, and Rhodopis seemed to know it, which is why she didn't pay much attention to what happened and continued to work.

The Pharaoh, who also knew who the eagle was, decided when the slipper fell on his lap that he would marry the owner since he believed it was a message from the gods. He traveled through Egypt via the Nile in search of the owner, until he reached the farm where Rhodopis was. The king's men, anxious to please him, just went inside and started trying the shoe on every female slave to see if it fits, which made her scared and so she hid.

When he was leaving, the Pharaoh spotted Rhodopis in her hiding place and told her to try on the slipper. She did, and it fit perfectly. She also removed the other slipper from her belongings, proving that the shoes were hers. It was then declared that she would be his queen and they immediately fell in love and got married.

Does this story remind you of any other? Well, if you said Cinderella, you are correct! This is the Ancient Egyptian version of the very famous fairy tale.

The Prince and the Sphinx

Thutmose was a prince of Egypt, son of Amenhotep, and grand-son of Hatshepsut. He was a very sad prince because, since he was the Pharaoh's favorite, everyone was always plotting against him. His brothers and step-brothers did this so that the king would not favor him anymore and would see him as unfit to become a ruler.

However, Thutmose was very smart and very skilled. In order to escape from these attempts, he would stay away from home as long as he could, even skipping important festivals in honor of the gods. One day, he decided to go hunting near the desert with two servants. They rode until they got to the Great

Pyramids of Giza, where Thutmose admired the structures. However, he saw that there was a head and part of a body coming from the sand, and identified it as being from the Sphinx.

The Sphinx started talking to him and said that he would be a great ruler and the prince, in exchange, said that once he became a Pharaoh, he would request that the parts of the structure that were buried in the sand be exposed again. He went back home and never again did anyone attempt to plot against him.

History said that he did in fact, become a pharaoh—one of the most successful—and that he fulfilled his promise to the Sphinx and built a temple at its feet in its honor.

The Princess of Bekhten

Once there was a pharaoh who was in the country of Nehern collecting taxes when a prince approached him and presented him with his eldest daughter as a gift. Since she was very beautiful, the pharaoh accepted her and named her Raneferu. However, years later, during a visit to the pharaoh, the father told the queen that her youngest sister was sick, and asked the pharaoh to send a doctor to see if they could help her.

When she was evaluated by the doctors, they came to the conclusion that she was sick because of an evil spirit. They called priests and other doctors, but the spirit would not leave the girl. The pharaoh did as requested and invoked the god Khonsu, sending a statue of him with some of his power. The god was able to release the evil spirit from the girl and she was cured.

Due to the power that he saw, the prince, the father of the girl, decided to keep the statue. The god stayed there for three years but decided to return to Egypt as a golden hawk. When the prince realized that the god was gone, he felt ashamed of his actions and sent the statue and a large number of offerings back. When everything arrived in Egypt, the pharaoh placed it in the Great Temple, at the foot of the statue of Khonsu.

The Peasant and the Workman

There once was a peasant who lived by selling goods from his country. One day, during his travels, he met a rich man who wished to the gods that he could steal all of the peasant's products and his wish was granted. After tricking the man, the rich man said that he was going to keep all of his products because no one would believe a poor peasant over a lord like him. The peasant cried and asked him not to do that, but it was useless.

The poor peasant then tried to look for justice, but no one would hear them. He wanted his belongings back after they were stolen and he had been beaten. The men of the court could not come to a decision and asked him to bring a witness, which he didn't have. The second time he went looking for justice, the king asked to provide his family with food and water without telling him where it came from.

The man kept coming back—for the third, fourth, fifth, and sixth time. Finally, at the ninth time, the king sent two men to speak to the lord, and the peasant was scared to be beaten again. However, the king had decided that the rich man should be removed from all of his titles and that all of his property be given to the peasant, who started to have a rich life and a good relationship with the family of the pharaoh.

The Tales of Rhampsinit

Rhampsinit was a very famous man in Egyptian stories. He was so popular that he was the main character in not one, but two Egyptian stories: one in which he is fooled by two thieves and the other when he visits Hades, the Lord of the underworld in Greek mythology. Even though he is portrayed as an Egyptian king, there is no record of a pharaoh with this name. Therefore, historians believe that he is a fictitious character, even though some versions of the story claim that the king was Ramses III. Shall we read these stories?

The King and the Thieves

King Rhampsinit was a very rich man who had a lot of gold, silver, and jewelry. Because of the value of his treasures, he wanted to build a safe room where he could store everything and keep it secure. He hired a master builder and his two sons to build this room and, after it was done, all his riches were placed inside. But the builder, who was not a very nice man, built a secret passage into the storage room and, when he was about to pass away, he told his sons about it.

The sons, greedy and want to have some of the riches, started entering the room in secret and stealing part of the king's riches. When the king noticed that part of his precious treasure was missing, he promised to get revenge and set many traps in the room, so that he could catch the thieves. One night, when the thieves were stealing the king's possessions, one of them stepped into the trap and was caught. Since he could not get away and feared that his brother would be caught, he asked to be left there, but that his brother cut off his head so that they would not be recognized.

The king was furious. Not only had they left with more of his treasure, but they were also smart enough not to be recognized. So, he says that there would be a prize to whoever identified the body. The mother of the two men, who found out about everything, begs her other son to get back the body of his brother so that he can have a proper burial. The man then disguises himself as a beggar, gives the guards wine to get them drunk, and steals the body. The king was even angrier, especially because the thief had outsmarted him.

But this story has a happy ending. In a last attempt to catch the men who were stealing from him, the king asks his daughter to help him to find out who the culprits are. She was so beautiful that the thief is enchanted by her but flees as soon as he realizes it is a trick. Finally, the king gave up and promised the hand of his daughter in marriage to the person who could prove that he was the thief. The thief presented himself and the king fulfilled his promise. The man and the princess got married and lived happily ever after.

King Rhampsinit Visits Hades

After King Rhampsinit died, he left the throne to his daughter's husband, the thief. Stories say that when he went to the underworld, he met Hades. Because he wanted to come back to the world of the living, he played dice with a goddess and won, which allowed him to come back. Happy because their king came back to them, the Egyptians celebrated a feast in his honor. A curiosity of this story is that at this time in Ancient Egypt, people used to throw dice to solve problems or make decisions.

The Sacred Lotus

The lotus is a flower that was filled with meaning for the Ancient Egyptians. But before I tell you more, I need to explain that this lotus was, in fact, what we know today as the water lily or the blue water lily, which has a yellow, golden-like center. Because of its importance, it was drawn in tombs in the hands of gods or humans, pottery was made resembling its shape, and many lotus flowers were scattered in the graves of the pharaohs when they passed away. Also, in Ancient Egypt, the lotus symbolized spiritual enlightenment.

In some myths, the flower rose from the water, in the beginning, to give origin to the sun or, in other stories, to the god Amun-Ra. The flower opened every morning for the god and closed at night, but he was lonely and wanted to share the world with other gods and people, so he created everything that exists. The way that the flower opens during the day and closes during the night is closely related to the myth created by the Egyptians.

One characteristic of the lily is that it has a very strong scent, so historians believe that it was probably used as perfume and as decoration at parties and festivals. Stories say that Cleopatra would take a bath every day with lotus flowers for their perfume. Still related to the scent, other myths claimed that the scent of the lily would bring people back from the dead, which is why there are so many pictures of people smelling them in Egyptian art.

Finally, the blue lily was represented in many other places in Ancient Egypt—they were in the jewelry men and women wore, in cups, in engravings, and in pottery artifacts. One of the findings in King Tutankhamun's tomb was a lotus chalice, which is in exhibition today for the public to see.

Monsters and Mythical Creatures of Ancient Egypt

Like so many other past cultures, Ancient Egypt also had its monsters and mythical creatures. They were mostly related to the gods and some kind of challenge that they would have to face. These creatures do not exist in reality, which is why they are called myths. People created them in order to symbolize something or to bring meaning to something that they did not understand. So, there is no reason to fear them, they are just part of a story!

Want to check some of them out? Come on!

Apep

As you have seen before, Apep was a serpent that the god Amun-Ra fought every night when he traveled to the underworld. But Apep was not just a normal serpent, it was a huge one! It was approximately 15 meters long and, because of its size, it caused earthquakes when it moved. But Amun-Ra wasn't the only god that fought the serpent. It also had an encounter with Set, which the Egyptians believed to be the origin of thunderstorms.

Uraeus

Contrary to the negative meaning that Apep has, the snake Uraeus was considered the cobra of the gods and symbolized the pharaohs' majesty. Do you know those tiaras that pharaohs are generally seen wearing in the drawings from Ancient Egypt? Well, if you look closely, you will see that it is a snake. And if you think that the snake represents Uraeus, you are absolutely right! It is the same representation, the only one that allowed a pharaoh to be recognized.

Bennu

Bennu was a self-created firebird related to Ra, very much like the phoenix, and it was a symbol of rebirth. Although the mythical bird became more known in Greek culture, it is believed that they borrowed the story from the Egyptians, since the Greek historian Herodotus claims in his writings that he was told about this specific bird during his travels to the country. It was initially drawn as a small bird but, later in history, was pictured as a huge animal with a long beak, similar to one that was native to the region but is now extinct.

The Griffin

The Griffin is a mythological creature that has the body of a lion and the wings and head of an eagle. It is generally used in Ancient Egyptian mythology to represent war since both animals that compose its body are hunters. It was also the guard of all the gods' treasures and can be seen pulling the chariots of the pharaohs in some of the period's drawings. Since the Griffin can also be found in other cultures, its origin is unknown.

CONCLUSION

Congratulations, you made it! You have reached the end of the book, and now you know a lot more about Ancient Egypt than many people. Here you have learned about the kingdoms, the country's geography, and what their life was like. Do you remember what the name of the important river in Egypt is—the one that is the largest in the world? The Nile! Yes! It was the Nile. The river was very important for the Egyptians and it allowed them to develop as a civilization. Of course, there was also the fact that Egypt is surrounded by desert, water, and mountains, which made it somewhat difficult for anyone to try to bother them while they moved on with their lives. Not that it didn't happen, but it took some time. Meanwhile, they were just there, creating, developing, and, of course, building pyramids!

You have learned a little bit more about the pharaohs, including the stories and traits of some of the most famous ones. Remember how cool it was to find out that King Tut's tomb was found almost untouched and that you can see everything that was inside? Would you have liked to be a king or a queen in Ancient Egypt? What do you think that was like? Do you think you would have enjoyed it? Well, I can say that I would, although I would be scared of having a cheetah as a pet or having to fight hippopotami in the Nile River. I guess you needed to be very smart and very brave to be a leader in Ancient Egypt. For sure you could have done it!

What about the gods and goddesses? You have learned about which ones were worshiped at the time, their stories and myths, and their relationships with each other. I know that it can be confusing with so many gods to keep track of—after all, there are over 2000—but I am sure that you have learned the main points about some of the most important. I think that gods and goddesses were really awesome. They had their magical powers, with which they could almost do as they please. Which god or goddess was your favorite?

There was also a part that talked about death and the afterlife in Ancient Egypt: You hung on like a brave hero and now you know a lot of neat things that they did when a loved one passed away—including building pyramids! Speaking of which, what did you think about the pyramids? Did you like learning more about them? Did you notice how many were built and how different they are from each other? The nice thing is that, if you want to, when you grow older you can go visit them and see them for yourself. That would be really neat!

Were you surprised by how many of the inventions made by the Egyptians we still use today? Can you remember all of them? I will help you start the list... toothbrush, door lock... can you name the others? I am sure that you can, and that you will now tell all of your friends about the cool things that you learned in this book. Who knows? Someday you might become an Egyptologist who discovers something new about the Egyptians, or you might even learn how to read hieroglyphs. I think it sounds like a great idea!

Finally came the most magical part of the book: the parts with the myths and stories. Did you see my surprise? Yes! I am talking about the first Cinderella story, which came directly from the Egyptians. Which was your favorite story? The one about the Book of Thoth, about the thieves, or about the Princess? What about the myths? Which one was your favorite? I bet you will always remember ancient Egypt every time you see a lily now.

I hope you enjoyed the book and know that it will be here, no matter how many times you want to read it and learn about Ancient Egypt. Goodbye!

REFERENCES

Adhikari, S. (2019, April 9). *Top 10 Fascinating Facts about the Egyptian Pyramids*. Ancient History Lists. https://www.ancienthistorylists.com/egypt-history/top-10-facts-egyptian-pyramids/

Allen, R. C. (1997). Agriculture and the Origins of the State in Ancient Egypt. *Explorations in Economic History, 34*(2), 135–154. https://doi.org/10.1006/exeh.1997.0673

Britannica. (2020). *Ancient Egypt - The Early Dynastic period* (c. 2925–c. 2575 bce). https://www.britannica.com/place/ancient-Egypt/The-Early-Dynastic-period-c-2925-c-2575-bce

Britannica. (2020). *Ancient Egypt - The Predynastic and Early Dynastic periods* https://www.britannica.com/place/ancient-Egypt/The-Predynastic-and-Early-Dynastic-periods

Ancient Egypt Online. (n.d.). *The Princess of Bekheten | Ancient Egypt Online*. https://ancientegyptonline.co.uk/princessbekheten/

Art in Context. (2021, July 14). *Egyptian Art - An Exploration of Ancient Egyptian Art and Its Influences*. https://artincontext.org/egyptian-art/

Arun. (2018, September 12). *10 Interesting Facts About Religion In Ancient Egypt | Learnodo Newtonic*. Learnodo-Newtonic.com. https://learnodo-newtonic.com/ancient-egypt-religion-facts

Atkins, H. (2018, June 20). *10 Famous Ancient Egyptian Pharaohs.* History Hit; History Hit. https://www.historyhit.com/famous-ancient-egyptian-pharaohs/

The Australian Museum. (2018, November 21). *Art in ancient Egypt.* https://australian.museum/learn/cultures/internatio nal-collection/ancient-egyptian/art-in-ancient-egypt/

Bevan, R. (n.d.). *The greatest pharaohs of Ancient Egypt.* Sky HISTORY TV Channel. Retrieved April 9, 2022, from https://www.history.co.uk/shows/legends-of-the-pharaohs/articles/the-greatest-pharaohs-of-ancient-egypt

The British Museum. (2017, August 2). *Everything you ever wanted to know about the Rosetta Stone.* The British Museum Blog; The British Museum. https://blog.britishmuseum.org/everything-you-ever-wanted-to-know-about-the-rosetta-stone/

Canadian Museum of History. (2019). *Egyptian civilization - Government.* Historymuseum.ca. https://www.historymuseum.ca/cmc/exhibitions/civi l/egypt/egcgov1e.html

Carnegie Museum of Natural History. (2020, September 14). *Egypt and the Nile.* https://carnegiemnh.org/egypt-and-the-nile/#:~:text=Ancient%20Egypt%20was%20located%20in

Chalmers, M. (2021, April 4). *Life after Death in Ancient Egypt | History Today.* Www.historytoday.com. https://www.historytoday.com/archive/history-matters/life-after-death-ancient-egypt

Digital Giza. (n.d.). *Daily Life in Ancient Egypt.* Giza.fas.harvard.edu; Harvard. Retrieved April 10, 2022, from http://giza.fas.harvard.edu/lessons/ancient-egyptian-writing

Dorman, P. F. (2019). Valley of the Kings | archaeological site, Egypt | Britannica. In *Encyclopædia Britannica.* https://www.britannica.com/place/Valley-of-the-Kings

Dorman, P. F., & Baines, J. R. (2017). ancient Egyptian religion | History, Rituals, & Gods. In *Encyclopædia Britannica.* https://www.britannica.com/topic/ancient-Egyptian-religion

Ducksters. (2019). *Ancient Egyptian History for Kids: Geography and the Nile River.* Ducksters.com. https://www.ducksters.com/history/ancient_egypt/geography_nile_river.php

Ducksters. (2019). *Ancient Egyptian History for Kids: Mummies.* https://www.ducksters.com/history/ancient_egyptian_mummies.php

Egyptian Myths. (2014). *Ancient Egypt: the Mythology - The Book of Thoth.* http://www.egyptianmyths.net/mythbookthoth.htm

Egyptian Myths. (n.d.). *Ancient Egypt: the Mythology - The Peasant and the Workman.* Www.egyptianmyths.net. Retrieved April 11, 2022, from http://www.egyptianmyths.net/mythsekhti.htm

Egyptian Myths. (n.d.). *Ancient Egypt: the Mythology - The Prince and the Sphinx*. Retrieved April 11, 2022, from http://www.egyptianmyths.net/mythsphinx.htm

Egyptian Myths. (n.d.). *Ancient Egypt: the Mythology - The Treasure Thief*. (2014). Egyptianmyths.net. http://www.egyptianmyths.net/mythtthief.htm

The Editors of Encyclopedia Britannica. (2019). *Book of the Dead | ancient Egyptian text*. https://www.britannica.com/topic/Book-of-the-Dead-ancient-Egyptian-text

The Editors of Encyclopaedia Britannica. (2019). *Egyptian architecture*. In Encyclopædia Britannica. https://www.britannica.com/art/Egyptian-architecture

The Editors of Encyclopaedia Britannica. (2018). *11 Egyptian Gods and Goddesses*. https://www.britannica.com/list/11-egyptian-gods-and-goddesses

The Editors of Encyclopedia Britannica. (2010). *Lower Egypt | geographical division, Egypt*. https://www.britannica.com/place/Lower-Egypt

The Editors of Encyclopedia Britannica. (2020). *Mortuary temple | Egyptian temple* https://www.britannica.com/topic/mortuary-temple

The Editors of Encyclopedia Britannica. (2020). *Mummy embalming*. https://www.britannica.com/topic/mummy

The Editors of Encyclopedia Britannica. (2016). *Pharaoh | Egyptian king*. https://www.britannica.com/topic/pharaoh

The Editors of Encyclopedia Britannica. (2019). *Pyramids of Giza | History & Facts.* https://www.britannica.com/topic/Pyramids-of-Giza

Eunice, M. (2019, January 14). *26 Strange Facts About The Pyramids Of Egypt Very Few Know.* TheTravel. https://www.thetravel.com/26-strange-facts-about-the-pyramids-of-egypt-very-few-know/

Flinders Petrie, W. M. (n.d.). *The Peasant and the Workman | TOTA.* Www.tota.world. Retrieved April 11, 2022, from https://www.tota.world/article/213/

Garnet, T., & Dorman, P. F. (2019). Egyptian art and architecture | History & Facts. In *Encyclopædia Britannica.* https://www.britannica.com/art/Egyptian-art

Handwerk, B. (2010, October 21). *Egypt's Valley of the Kings Provides a Window to the Past.* History. https://www.nationalgeographic.com/history/article/valley-of-the-kings

Handwerk, B. (2017, January 21). *Pyramids of Giza | National Geographic.* History. https://www.nationalgeographic.com/history/article/giza-pyramids

Hays, J. (n.d.). *WORSHIP AND RITUALS IN ANCIENT EGYPT | Facts and Details.* Factsanddetails.com. Retrieved April 9, 2022, from https://factsanddetails.com/world/cat56/sub403/entry-6114.html

Heritage Daily. (2021, January 19). *The Ancient Egyptian Pyramids.*

https://www.heritagedaily.com/2021/01/the-ancient-egyptian-pyramids/134365

History for Kids. (2019). *Animals of Ancient Egypt - Facts for Kids.* https://www.historyforkids.net/egyptian-animals.html

History on the Net. (2018, April 25). *Egyptian Social Classes and Society - History.* https://www.historyonthenet.com/the-egyptians-society

History.com Editors. (2018, August 21). *Egyptian Pyramids.* HISTORY; A&E Television Networks. https://www.history.com/topics/ancient-history/the-egyptian-pyramids

History.com Editors. (2020, February 21). *Ancient Egypt.* HISTORY; A&E Television Networks. https://www.history.com/topics/ancient-history/ancient-egypt

Hoch, J. (2019). Egyptian language | History, Writing, & Hieroglyphics. In *Encyclopædia Britannica.* https://www.britannica.com/topic/Egyptian-language

HowStuffWorks. (2021, December 16). *10 Amazing Ancient Egyptian Inventions.* https://science.howstuffworks.com/innovation/inventions/5-amazing-ancient-egyptian-inventions.htm

Hughes, T. (2019, October 30). *13 Important Gods and Goddesses of Ancient Egypt.* History Hit. https://www.historyhit.com/important-gods-and-goddesses-of-ancient-egypt/

Jarus, O. (2012, September 10). *Step Pyramid of Djoser: Egypt's First Pyramid*. Live Science; Live Science. https://www.livescience.com/23050-step-pyramid-djoser.html

Kasawne, S. (n.d.). *Myth Project: The Treasure Thief*. Sites.google.com. Retrieved April 11, 2022, from https://sites.google.com/site/mythprojectthetreasuret hief/

Kashyap Vyas. (2018, February 25). *Egyptian pyramids have been fascinating us since long. Despite a lot of research, there are still many secrets*. Interestingengineering.com; Interesting Engineering. https://interestingengineering.com/explore-33-interesting-facts-about-the-ancient-egyptian-pyramids

Kiger, P. J. (2021, July 26). *8 Facts About Ancient Egypt's Hieroglyphic Writing*. HISTORY. https://www.history.com/news/hieroglyphics-facts-ancient-egypt

Kinnaer, J. (2013). *Bent Pyramid at Dashur | The Ancient Egypt Site*. Ancient-Egypt.org. http://www.ancient-egypt.org/history/old-kingdom/4th-dynasty/snofru/pyramids/bent-pyramid-at-dashur.html

Mark, J. (2009, September 2). *Pharaoh*. World History Encyclopedia. https://www.worldhistory.org/pharaoh/

Mark, J. (2016a, January 18). *Predynastic Period in Egypt*. World History Encyclopedia. https://www.worldhistory.org/Predynastic_Period_i n_Egypt/

Mark, J. (2016b, January 20). *Ancient Egyptian Religion.* World History Encyclopedia. https://www.worldhistory.org/Egyptian_Religion/

Mark, J. (2016c, January 22). *Early Dynastic Period In Egypt.* World History Encyclopedia. https://www.worldhistory.org/Early_Dynastic_Period_In_Egypt/

Mark, J. (2016d, March 18). *Pets in Ancient Egypt.* World History Encyclopedia. https://www.worldhistory.org/article/875/pets-in-ancient-egypt/#:~:text=The%20ancient%20Egyptians%20kept%20animals

Mark, J. (2016e, March 28). *Egyptian Afterlife - The Field of Reeds.* World History Encyclopedia. https://www.worldhistory.org/article/877/egyptian-afterlife---the-field-of-reeds/

Mark, J. (2016f, April 14). *Egyptian Gods - The Complete List.* World History Encyclopedia. https://www.worldhistory.org/article/885/egyptian-gods---the-complete-list/

Mark, J. (2016g, September 26). *Old Kingdom of Egypt.* World History Encyclopedia. https://www.worldhistory.org/Old_Kingdom_of_Egypt/

Mark, J. (2016h, October 13). *Ancient Egyptian Government.* World History Encyclopedia. https://www.worldhistory.org/Egyptian_Government/#:~:text=The%20government%20of%20ancient%20Egypt

Mark, J. (2017a, January 10). *Ancient Egyptian Agriculture.* World History Encyclopedia. https://www.worldhistory.org/article/997/ancient-egyptian-agriculture/

Mark, J. (2017b, June 15). *Trade in Ancient Egypt*. World History Encyclopedia. https://www.worldhistory.org/article/1079/trade-in-ancient-egypt/

Menes | Pharaoh, Accomplishments, Definition, History, & Facts | Britannica. (n.d.). Www.britannica.com. Retrieved April 9, 2022, from https://www.britannica.com/biography/Menes#:~:text=Menes%2C%20also%20spelled%20Mena%2C%20Meni

Millmore, M. (2007, December 31). *Ancient Egyptian Gods and Goddesses.* Discovering Ancient Egypt. https://discoveringegypt.com/ancient-egyptian-gods-and-goddesses/

Millmore, M. (2008, January 1). *Ancient Egyptian Inventions.* Discovering Ancient Egypt. https://discoveringegypt.com/ancient-egyptian-inventions/

Ministry of Tourism and Antiquities. (n.d.). *The Red Pyramid.* Egymonuments.gov.eg. Retrieved April 9, 2022, from https://egymonuments.gov.eg/monuments/the-red-pyramid/

Ministry of Tourism and Antiquities. (n.d.). *Valley of the Kings.* Retrieved April 11, 2022, from https://egymonuments.gov.eg/archaeological-sites/valley-of-the-kings/

National Geographic. (2021, July 16). *How the Rosetta Stone unlocked the secrets of ancient civilizations.* https://www.nationalgeographic.com/history/article/how-the-rosetta-stone-unlocked-the-secrets-of-ancient-civilizations

Nix, E. (2018, August 23). *What is the Rosetta Stone?* HISTORY. https://www.history.com/news/what-is-the-rosetta-stone

Reading Museum. (2020, May 11). *Sacred animals of Ancient Egypt.* Reading Museum. https://www.readingmuseum.org.uk/blog/sacred-animals-ancient-egypt

Reuters. (2019, July 14). *"Bent" pyramid: Egypt opens ancient oddity for tourism.* The Guardian; The Guardian. https://www.theguardian.com/world/2019/jul/14/bent-pyramid-egypt-opens-ancient-oddity-for-tourism

Smithsonian. (2012). *Egyptian Mummies.* Smithsonian Institution. https://www.si.edu/spotlight/ancient-egypt/mummies

Smithsonian. (2019). *The Egyptian Pyramid.* Smithsonian Institution. https://www.si.edu/spotlight/ancient-egypt/pyramid

Society, N. G. (2019, March 1). *Pharaohs.* National Geographic Society. https://www.nationalgeographic.org/encyclopedia/pharaohs/#:~:text=As%20ancient%20Egyptian%20rulers%2C%20pharaohs

Storynory. (2021, May 16). *The Doomed Prince.* https://www.storynory.com/the-doomed-prince/

Students of History. (n.d.). *Ancient Egypt's Geography*. Retrieved April 10, 2022, from https://www.studentsofhistory.com/ancient-egypt-s-geography

Thompson, S. (2021, July 2). *Ten Facts on the Ancient Egyptian Pyramids*. Blog.bridgemanimages.com. https://blog.bridgemanimages.com/blog/ten-facts-on-the-ancient-egyptian-pyramids

Tikkanen, A. (2017). Great Sphinx of Giza | Description, History, & Facts. In *Encyclopædia Britannica*. https://www.britannica.com/topic/Great-Sphinx

UShistory. (2019). *Egyptian Social Structure [ushistory.org]*. https://www.ushistory.org/civ/3b.asp

Wendorf, M. (2019, April 23). *Ancient Egyptian Technology and Inventions*. Interestingengineering.com. https://interestingengineering.com/ancient-egyptian-technology-and-inventions#:~:text=The%20ancient%20Egyptians%20would%20come

WorldAtlas. (2016, October 5). *Ancient Egyptian Animals*. WorldAtlas. https://www.worldatlas.com/articles/animals-of-ancient-egypt.html

OTHER BOOKS BY HISTORY BROUGHT ALIVE

- Mythology for Kids: Explore Timeless Tales, Characters, History, & Legendary Stories from Around the World. Norse, Celtic, Roman, Greek, Egypt & Many More

Available now on Kindle, Paperback, Hardcover & Audio in all regions

- Greek Mythology For Kids: Explore Timeless Tales & Bedtime Stories From Ancient Greece. Myths, History, Fantasy & Adventures of The Gods, Goddesses, Titans, Heroes, Monsters & More

Available now on Kindle, Paperback, Hardcover & Audio in all regions

- Norse Mythology for Kids: Legendary Stories, Quests & Timeless Tales From Norse Folklore. The Myths, Sagas & Epics of The Gods, Immortals, Magic Creatures, Vikings & More

Available now on Kindle, Paperback, Hardcover & Audio in all regions

FREE BONUS FROM HBA: EBOOK BUNDLE

Greetings!

First of all, thank you for reading our books. As fellow passionate readers of History and Mythology, we aim to create the very best books for our readers.

Now, we invite you to join our VIP list. As a welcome gift, we offer the History & Mythology Ebook Bundle below for free. Plus you can be the first to receive new books and exclusives! Remember it's 100% free to join.

Simply scan the QR code to join.

Keep up to date with us on:

YouTube: History Brought Alive

Facebook: History Brought Alive

www.historybroughtalive.com